Roma

**Roma**
Bernard Saint

Smokestack Books
1 Lake Terrace, Grewelthorpe, Ripon HG4 3BU
e-mail: info@smokestack-books.co.uk
www.smokestack-books.co.uk

Text copyright 2016,
Bernard Saint,
all rights reserved.

ISBN 978-0-9931490-7-8

Smokestack Books is represented
by Inpress Ltd

*I would like to express my gratitude to Anne Beresford who first heard this book in its making.*

*And to Elis Pehkonen who facilitated its performance in the William Alwyn Festival.*

*To my father*

# Contents

| | |
|---|---|
| Bestiarii | 9 |
| Bella Figura | 10 |
| Transformer | 11 |
| A Roman in Umbria | 13 |
| Tribute to Marcus Aurelius | 14 |
| 'Bust of Marcus Aurelius as a Boy' | 15 |
| Julian's Dilemma | 16 |
| Marcus Aurelius at the Theatre | 17 |
| 'Quiet on the Set' | 19 |
| Amphorae | 20 |
| Marcus Aurelius on the Catwalk | 21 |
| Sailing for Lindos | 24 |
| Campagna | 26 |
| Song of the Bees | 27 |
| Marcus Aurelius & the Cult of Celebrity | 28 |
| Photo-Shoot | 30 |
| Showbiz Plus – Marcus Meets Celeb – All the Goss | 32 |
| Sunbathing Pope | 34 |
| Orpheus – Son of Apollo | 36 |
| Porta Magica | 37 |
| Strolling through Rome with Marcus Aurelius | 38 |
| Chet Baker in Bologna | 40 |
| A Messenger | 41 |
| Surveillance in Full View | 42 |
| Marcus Aurelius: Sixties Icon | 44 |
| European Tour | 45 |
| Marcus Aurelius Discourses on Vintage Guitars | 46 |
| Marcus Aurelius Rehab | 47 |
| Marcus Aurelius and the Chinese Trade Delegation | 48 |
| Rest & Recreation | 50 |
| Bathing at Baden | 51 |
| Roman Leave | 52 |
| Marcus Aurelius: Mentor | 53 |
| The Games | 55 |
| Marcus Aurelius at the Cenotaph | 56 |

| | |
|---|---:|
| Marcus Aurelius: A Long Campaign | 57 |
| Gregory's Corso | 59 |
| Villa Borghese | 61 |
| Idioms of March | 62 |
| The Spanish Steps | 63 |
| Marcus Aurelius: Historian | 64 |
| Marcus Aurelius is from Mars | 65 |
| Conquest | 66 |
| One Small Room | 67 |
| Spiritus | 68 |
| Men at Work | 69 |
| Excavation | 70 |
| Marcus Aurelius: On Love | 71 |
| A Foreign Country | 73 |
| Drusilla | 74 |
| Patrol | 76 |
| Policy Application | 77 |
| The Temple at Jerusalem | 78 |
| Marcus Aurelius: Astronomer | 79 |
| Chet: 'Summer Sketch' | 80 |
| Maggiore | 81 |
| Marcus Aurelius: On Impiety | 82 |
| The Animals Preach to St. Francis | 83 |
| Fontana | 84 |
| Duchessa | 85 |
| Paper Dagger | 86 |
| Marcus Aurelius is Not Proud | 87 |
| Prolific | 89 |
| Bay of Lindos | 90 |
| A Provincial Assizes | 91 |
| Cinecitta | 92 |
| Marcus Aurelius Offers Solace | 93 |
| Marcus Aurelius: Webpage | 95 |

# Bestiarii

One elephant has wrapped her dying
Infant in her trunk
Then raising him
Above the mangled sand
Will not relinquish him

To these dismaying men
Slip sandaled in her gore

Trident bearers   hammer men
Javelin   and axemen

For these uneasy predators
The Coliseum hurls
A net ominous and silent

The crowd are on their feet
They are facing down the Emperor's prerogative
Demanding end to this un-Roman show

It is clear who has nobility
Who not –

Remembering a she-wolf suckled Rome
The fierce implacable mother
Primal as the cosmos in us all

She it is who stands in her own blood
Roaring from her depths
'My son   my son'

And in that moment Trajan fell from power

# Bella Figura

Search me what women see
In well-honed hunks
Their trunks too tight and torsos strained
To requisite charcuterie
For gladiatorial games –
Perhaps some dames incline by their desire
To be soft-centre of a rugby scrum

But I am just an old and decadent poet
I murmur one 'bon mot'
Then salon to salon the same
Boredom of abandoned luxury offends me –
So I take my afternoon tea
With the wonderful Sisters of Mercy
Who raise their veils for me
Emboldened by our long platonic friendship

Glimpses of a transcendental beauty
Invoke in us an ardent chastity –

Who else might tolerate you ask
My languid and emaciated frame?
My desiccated and ironic diction?
Those who persist to retain
A broken but lyrical valour

Well this is the price you pay
When the muses secretly smile
While bestowing toxic laurel
On one who was a boy – and fully unprepared
For *their* long game of hazard

If there's a chance you hear beyond the Shade
Now isn't this so my beauties?

## Transformer

When I grow tired of the modern world
I turn into an olive tree
And trickle my roots to first century wells
In the Mediterranean basin

I sit beneath my silvery leaves
The kernel of my being
An ancient olive stone
Resilient and persistent

Olive arms and faces
Long -faded from your frescoes
Enjoy the grace and silence of my shade –
Poets scribble half a dozen lines
The future will insist are but a fragment
Of epics dispersed and lost
To sandstorms of antiquity –
Then dine on honeyed dormice
At the court of Vespasian

Mindful a man declines
Merchants' lonely daughters
Sweetmeats sold inside the public circus
Political office and loaded dice
He may live to see his fortieth winter –
When Fate may try to fit him up again
In the role of an Uxbridge solicitor –
For he has lost his concentration
Growing tired of antiquity –

The spitted oxen stuffed with calf and lamb and piglet sausage
The swan containing goose containing fowl and snipe and quail –
Time itself is composed of conflated features –
A distended indigestible telescope

You modernists may keep your century –
We'll mingle with you on a weekend break
You'll greet us at the baths or in the gym
The pizza parlour   festival   and wine-bar –
Inheriting our pastimes and our pleasures
You'll scandalise our brief amoral lives –
You cannot see  *you are immersed in them*

# A Roman in Umbria

Having enjoyed all pleasures of the flesh
The young delight to exaggerate
Having endured all pleasures of the flesh
That render an old man asinine
I retire to my three-walled estate
An olive farm entertained
By bears and wolves
Who vandalise my crop by night
One week before it's harvested

I shall endure these winters
Imagining my friends
Around my fire of half-sawn logs –
Those who kicked the bucket down the well
Not noticing their ankles
Tangled in its chain

I notice now
Early frost and chill
Herbs and flowers struggling
Clinging to existence –

Another patch of sun
Apollo if you please

Let them remember forest birds
Gathering green stalks
The music of the bees
Amid their cornucopia of seed

# Tribute to Marcus Aurelius

Long ago it seemed
The city did not circulate by money –
You occupied poor quarters nonetheless
Jobs and bed-sits few would countenance

With poetry your permanent companion –
So a boy of seventeen might estimate
Hope and inspiration
Sacredly above the prudent mind

Regarding sober stoics who maintained
There is one trusted guardian at best
Dwells within your house when all grows dark
You lacked both chronic need and inclination

You craved the muses' food of mere seduction
A storm-fly pressed against their windowpane
You turned aside from knowledge to those passions
Whose false-reflected pleasures twitched your wings

## 'Bust of Marcus Aurelius as a Boy'

Who is this modernist?
His beardless face
His curls too artfully trimmed
By Sassoon on via Veneto?

I hardly recognise myself –
He seems a kind of youth
Impelled to pretty writing
One who can't abstain from poetry

Appearances are wonderful
Misleaders of sound reason
All modernists knew this –
The girl-boys on Lambrettas
Their boy-girls lolling stylishly at pillion

Their stories fade
Then turn to myth
And though you break your heart
The world runs on as before

This boy might seem too slight a soul
To lug about two corpses
One of course his own
The other his dead father

Transformed to ghostly mentor
Father drives him on
To seek the truth as Shakespeare's Danish prince
Who found court life contemptible

Then perusing his late Jester's jaw
Upturned from its grave
He contemplated this –

Death smiles at us all –
All you may do is   *smile back*

## Julian's Dilemma

In this distracting and extravagant city
A man must wear a plausible mask to survive

A young man it is imagined
Still has straw in his hair
Providing his demeanour
Remains sufficiently modest

So he endures this tedium
Copying legal documents in the Senate

When really he might assume
A role in sunlit processions
Orating his startling verse in Nero's presence

But then – exposed to jealousies
Of jackals who draw unscrupulous pay
Denouncing all that's new as insurrection
Implicating unprotected citizens as spies…

Literature is not an easy passage
It fuels neurotic ache for recognition

And at this most dangerous time
The Empire a paranoid beehive

With access to the records of the Senate
What state secrets might he stand accused of leaking?

## Marcus Aurelius at the Theatre

Every vice of our delusion
Amplified by an actor's mask

I'd sooner stay at home
Sipping *espresso e aqua*
In my corner pavement café
Though this is not a bolt-hole
From the theatre

These passers-by
Surely they are extras
From sword and sandal epics –
Always clad in Armani
They stroll about in a bubble
Of self-dramatising soap

When did the world
Become like this
A playground
For the narcissist?

Self-publicists
Outweigh good sense
Preening on the internet

Then from a corner of your home
Reality T. V
Distracts you from reality

If they should make me Caesar
I will not become 'a Caesar'
But elude the dipping in purple dye
That amplifies all character
Then like an actor's mask
Inflates the smallest defect

I'll keep my rough Greek cloak
And reject the duck-down pallet
When I choose to sleep on the floor

## 'Quiet on the Set'

'Now you turn to him a long look of regret
Wordless yet   anticipating this
The audience must know –
You are of royal blood
Romance cannot be realised
But always  *always*   you shall remember Rome –

The freedom of the senses
Of which the masses drink their fill
In this exhilarating and intoxicating city
Free of royal obligation
Free of abstract duty and duress

And furthermore – I do not wish
To hear your private conversation
Your words of woe
Ingratitude   opinion
Keep these for the movie magazines –

The hardship of Los Angeles
Of stardom cruelly scrutinised
Struggles of a childhood
Save all this
When you phone your psychoanalyst

We are making a happy picture
A happy family picture
With Rome our glamour backdrop
And furthermore our budget overdue'

# Amphorae

Take these terracotta flasks
Their stoppers gone
But narrow necks intact
Found beneath Etruscan tiles –
The floor of an ancient villa
Turned up in our tenuous search
For further tube-train routes –

When each new find necessitates
A compromise of track
We call in double-quick
Crack troops of archaeologists

Who deliberate   pronouncing our containers
Amphorae pertaining
To unguents and perfumes
Requisites for a Roman bath
Brought onto the mezzanine when needed

This being so   we gave them fitting names –
'L'Atrine'   'Eau de Toilet'
'Gorillas in a Mist'
Just take a whiff of this –

We speculate the later Howard Hughes
Was not the first magnate
To develop obsessive traits
Urophiliac in nature –

While wealth and power expressed themselves in cultivated gardens
Which even those in debt might build beyond the city gates

Hoarding from his Fate our ancient miser
Stored waste product of his corporate body
In ritual to Croesus – a Netherworld of wealth

# Marcus Aurelius on the Catwalk

Meeting Marcus Aurelius at *Bar Zero*
That fashionistas' hangout on Bologna's main piazza
Where media Italians shop for leisure and for labels
Foraging its shaded porticoes
We remark how little fashion ever changes –
Prioritising youth's ephemeral beauty
Applying its discretions to those advanced in years
Its acolytes remaining unconstrained
By studies of a philosophic nature
That only tone *the mind*
When one has aged

Money   Power   Success and Pleasure
These remain its mantra from conception
That one might wear an outer show
Of attributes insensible to virtue –
Even dress that deviates
Soon finds assimilation
To high style –
So *Punk* and *Grunge* parade now in gold clasps
And safety pins of platinum will have you max. your plastic
In purchasing your daughter her contemporary demeanour

When we were young we had the uniform
Some called *bohemian* –
It was a uniform for non-conformists
Unquestioning   we rigidly conformed
Else we might never
Recognise each other
Holding as we did diverse ideas
Maturity then ripened into seeds expelled from pods
Our separate ways to sow and walk alone

Then little did we know
Nor should we guess
Our future days –
Of sensible supportive footwear
Ergonomic chairs
Our regimens of pills and
The elasticated waistband…

But I digress – it was the Roman hedonist
Gave birth to our most venerated models –
Anorexia Nervosa and her twin
Bulimia I see
Haunting constantly the vomitorium
Their perpetual cigarettes
Preserving pearl-like European pallor

Do you realise I dined once with a model?
Her photographs superbly draped
The glossy leaves of *Vanity* and *Vogue*
But in the flesh – my gods – appeared a fright
Her pitchfork limbs and bulbous eyes evoked
A range of famine   pogrom   and addiction
I swear I lost my appetite
So like herself I pushed – about a mile –
Two spinach leaves around my dinner plate
And found no room for pasta

No doubt you've seen Fellini's parody –
The Ecclesiastical Catwalk?
Kinetic head-dressed anchorites
Entering on roller-skates
Circle an audience of dowagers
While skeletons from catacombs parade
Cobwebbed and crumbling to dust –
So my fascination for this clothes-horse
Had its touch of horror

Aurelius – though you profess
Not the slightest interest in fashion –
Surely there had come a day you found
Your rough Greek cloak of wool
An affectation?
Put aside the tweeds and corduroys
We might advise the modern thinker
Seek out those master tailors
Peppino Scarapazzi
Giorgio Battistoni –
Creators of 'the simple and the good' Italian suit –
A future time may come to call it *Mod* –
Though men forget its elegance
Entirely stems from Roman Stoic values

# Sailing for Lindos

I am tired of this modern religion
Lolling around in pools   surrounded by starlets
Selling us lotions and serums
Comparing our hair-weaves and face-lifts
With senators and actors
Sponsoring aphrodisiac vascular enhancers –
I find it too frivolous   too desperate
And Destiny has told me
This is no occupation for a Roman poet

I hate their temples serving lamb and veal
Perpetually feasting –
To sacrifice the young of any species
Weighs me with remorse
Old carnivorous men   should not recline on cushions
Their recreational stimulants and sherbets
Get right up my nose

Complacently our culture is unravelling –
Orators perform their wares
Only to the comic muse
You ask them for the classics
Their lips become a trout's
Eyes dilate and dart about
Their repertoire dumbed-down beyond recalling

Why should I like the Games
Their chariot wheels contrived
To make a steak tartare of every rival?
We see enough barbarity
Simply setting foot outside our homes
When macho-men make hells of weekend revels
And women by skilled flatterers descend to turpitude

In brief I'm forced to flee these thriving stews –
Let others be inspired by their inconsequential clamour
I've made up my mind soon to set sail
For the lonely Greek isles of 'the nameless god'
Since other deities derive from man's perdition
Only poetry is where
You never hope to find her –
Transacting business in that land
Between myth and dream and mathematics

# Campagna

Traveller   what you are seeking
Is so often to be found
Not ten yards from your home

Though you circle the world to find it
All shall be waiting here
For your return –

Unremarkable soil
It hardly yields a thing
Except desire to leave

But someday you may treasure
Its lack of misleading promises
Its distance from the dissolute great cities

## Song of the Bees

They say the proud
Are reborn as bees

'I am an important painter'
'I am a superlative chef'
'I am an eminent senator'
'Just so' the proud man says

Then since he will not turn to prayer
Believing no brief illness
To be entirely final

He joins the ones reborn as bees
Murmuring over and over
'I am'   'I am'   'I am'

# Marcus Aurelius & the Cult of Celebrity

Observe the kind of mind that chases fame –
A ship cannot rely on one small sail
A life cannot sustain by one ambition –
Self-serving man sustains a little while
Until his sea of arrogance subsumes him

Your envy will outlive all happiness
Of those whom you believe are held above you –
But court dissatisfaction with your lot
Many form from this well-paid professions –

The cynical psychologists who claim
'Everything is what you think it is'
Carving up the words of Epictetus
To suit their busy bromides
Reducing to banality
His vision of the unity of all things

The world is filled with nature's refugees
In exile from the heart as from the soul
Yet dedicate a little time
To those few things you need
To suit a Roman and a man
Of independent dignity
Considering the cosmos
A single living being

Your life is but a moment
Do not set your happiness to waver
On flattery or censure of some other –
Only seek the company of those
With whom your capabilities expand

This narrow ledge we walk some call 'alive' –
Enticed with promises of pleasure
Constrained by alternating thoughts of pain –
How cheap and how corruptible –
Whose judgements and opinions
Confer renown on a harried rock?

One who sets his sights on fame
And while obscure endures the dream
Of posthumous recognition –
The praise of all the world
Means nothing to the dead
The living who remember him
One by one resume oblivion

Memory and fame are this
A rock-pool between tides
While ceaselessly the river meets the sea

# Photo-Shoot

So harmless seem their sugar-coated questions
Assuring all is surface with a style
Only stars possess in such abundance
Cameras whirr and purr and click and skirl

A fawn steps from her forest
Blinking in white headlines
Of a six-lane motorway –
Their magazines devoted to the movies

And so the hunt begins –
The private lives of actors
Their hedonistic searchlight
Stuns then overwhelms

When young and newly famous
Unbounded speculation
Reassures a readership
Talent and attainment are mere luck
Salacious gossip then
Appears not envious
But worldly well-informed…

When should one hostile journalist
Summarily decide
You are a 'difficult' subject
Her jangling hangover
Stumbling on the parquet
Spills bilious opinion into print

Then fuming at your gate
A pack of them pursuing on Lambrettas

Go stake your first long paycheck
On a souped-up mini cooper
Darken all the windows –
Tutored by a diamond-heist technician
Drive for all you're worth

Upon their rooftops autograph 'faint praise' in grey exhaust

# Showbiz Plus – Marcus Meets Celeb – All the Goss

'Unseemly scenes –
Old Sober Sides
Gadding about by night
Confirming hands-on interest
In our hot new telly siren –

'Kissing and entwining' someone said –
OK – perhaps a peck on either cheek –
But that's quite 'rock 'n' roll' where he resides!

Sabbia Mobili was back in town
Granting sound-bites for her latest series –
Your fave celeb-reporter ran amok
Loading up on freebies at the Launch
When who should he slide into
Propping up a pillar at the Bash
But Marcus 'I lend gravitas' Aurelius

'We're just good friends' Madonna Mobili said
'Unfortunately I gotta paira boobs
So some would put together two and two
Just to scribble paparazzi lies' –
In Sabbia's swanky uptown hotel suite
She said 'I love your Roman art and culture'
And though she goes for action over text
Would like to star in 'something by De Sica'
'Providing the right vehicle can be found'

A fitness freak she once passed out
In the midst of a Cranberry Cleanse – and warned
'It can crash an eager dieter's metabolism'

'Marco' – as I know him – added this
'Miss Mobili adapts our Ancient Rome
To popular acclaim –
Re-names it 'Dallas'
Retaining some reversals and betrayals
Power-games and family dynamics
Intrigues scandals and suspicious deaths
That make it still the hallmark
Of a moral civilization'

Meanwhile those cult refuseniks 'Church of Christ'
Claim love alone can bring the dead to life –
Follow me on Twitter for updates'

# Sunbathing Pope

August is a microwave
Only holy fools
Or tourists brave the heat

He boards a bus on Termini
Sabbatical professors
Burdened by their cameras
Baseball caps and bum-bags
Turning from their guidebooks
Offer Him a seat

Whose parish is the world
The same we glimpse
From public transport windows
Worried about bills
Even as we travel on to work

And contemplate a city that emerges
Continuous as Venus from the sea

Today He comes to bless
The shining orchard of retired
Sunbathing Cinecitta stars
Toasting on their terraces

'Here is a trellis your Holiness
Be sure to sit in the shade'
But no –
Centuries of heavy vestments
Confining protocols and paraphernalia –
It is time for a new dispensation

So send out for a pizza
While He anoints both legs and arms
In Cocoa Butter factor 25
Before some passing cardinal
Instantly envelops Him
In figured cloth of gold

'*You* may wear it monsignor –
The carnival is over'

# Orpheus – Son of Apollo

Roman Orpheus
Bear your lamb from harm
Protector of the lost and newly-born
This tender creature draped upon
Your adolescent shoulder
The only princely mantle you lay down

To frolic with the nightingales and fishes
Concordant yet transcending nature's power
Your simple tunic boasts
No purple trim – authority
Lives only in the grace-notes of your lyre

One naked foot is pierced
By time's narcotic thorn
But your eyes see all too clear –
And so the ikon-makers shall suggest
Your candid poet's face
A pattern of harmonic countenance
Beneath the un-recorded face of Christ –

'The Good Shepherd' you become – also
'The Harrower of Hell' –

Where hides that wounded fawn Eurydice
Your shy Byzantine princess?
'Don't look back' – she has become
In semblance of her bridal fresco
The numinous white flame of the Holy Virgin –

South of Tiber's sage-green trailing ribbon
Fountains   groves of olives   lemon gardens
Are her veil

## Porta Magica

Peeling arcades and market-stall mounds
Of cheap leather satchels sandals and shoes
Empire of junk-jewels   second-hand clothes
This is Piazza Vittorio

But go between carts of freshly-cut flowers
Into the park that once was a meadow
Find in its green meticulous ruin
One early Roman fountain

Then this mysterious standing door
Inscribed by alchemical symbols
Secure behind a black-barred surround
So only stray cats can enjoy it

What is alchemy
If once in modest majesty
God as infant lay on straw?
He did not turn this into spun-gold thread –

But Sweden's Queen Christina
Roman Rosicrucian poets
Tested every medieval manuscript
To find the Philosopher's Stone

Garlands of green amaranth
Became their votive symbol
This rigorous *Work* absorbed their lives
But were their hearts so pure?

Hermetic knowledge for today –
I stand at *Zeno's* bright zinc bar
Ordering a coloured strip of tickets –
It's just a tram ride after all
To pass through Rome's eternal
Fourth dimensional door
And be transformed forever

# Strolling through Rome with Marcus Aurelius

Why *do* all statues fit me with a beard?
Reduce me to an ideal cast in bronze?
'Aurelius: he's always on campaign
Philosopher and Guardian of Rome –
Therefore he never shaves' – they might well say
'He never bathes'

Give me a break!
Don't take me for a Pict!
Forget my highbrow youth –
A little prig
Immersed in esoteric Grecian thought
Might *then* try out a pipe and train his stubble

But I'm a human being first and last –
Everything you've heard
Is mere opinion not a fact
Everything described
Perspective not the truth

Quality of thought – that's all
We ever might possess –
Then give this to the public good
Expecting nothing back –

Sunday afternoons I take
A walk to *Port' Portese* –
That market five miles long
A narrow track
Jammed with bargain hunters
*Bric-a-brac* and stalls

You want a single bicycle clip?
Perhaps you lost its brother?
Here you find a surrogate –
Do you collect
Bottle tops from pop
Quenched your grandad's thirst
In brands long years defunct?

You'll find no item wasted
Nor hear this great bazaar
Described as arrant trash

Likewise we human beings
Find fulfilment simply being –
Life will have its use of us
When we give up connoisseurship
For simplicity

## Chet Baker in Bologna

Concerning Chet Baker my lips are sealed
By a calm vermilion glowing coal
At the centre of a snowball –
This was his sound – his soul

A snowflake turning to a flame mid –air
A cool conduit concluding
In a candlelit basilica –

The groove above our upper lip
A fingertip impresses before birth
Advises silence on our true abode –

'Hush   this is the world
Which shall pass
Though music last' –

To contemplate at lowered microphone
A whispered existential question mark
That bends his reputation to a stance

Of *spretzatura* understated cool –
Articulation of the difficult
Without personal bravura

# A Messenger

Let me tell you about the gods –
They keep honey where you keep salt
And salt where you keep honey

That is why
There is nowhere on earth to hide from them

They prefer the prayers of children –
That if anyone abuse them
So then they cease to pray

A messenger is sent to hear their silence
Investigate the vortex
Of impacted threnody

Let me tell you about the gods –
Their slow implacable justice

# Surveillance in Full View

'Sip a cappuccino now the sun is on the roof
That way you're sure to pass here for a tourist

Then tell me who's 'Fellini' anyway
That he presumes to spy on us
Passing freely from our time to his
When meeting here to laugh at each 'improvement'?

He's seeking invitation to the orgies?
Don't slop your froth like that!
I really think this is no joking matter –

Pasolini told him   'Federico   how'd I know?
I'm not *bourgeois*   I *never* go to orgies!'

His subterfuge is deeper one suspects –
A Jungian analyst warned him
We the archetypes
Are not some petty Tinkerbells to mess with –
You'd think he'd heed such counsel
Adopting our discretion of *omerta*

Suppose our sacred vehicle
Poetry – impounded here in time –
Fell to the hands of anarchists?
They'd filter its fuel into fountains
Mountain springs maligned immodest Nero
Pipelined into Roma city centre –

Then all the world might sing and run amuck
Freed of time's immobilising tyranny –
For now they think they are
Units of production chained
As slaves to their factory clock

Do you suppose they are ready for
*Free Time*?

'Fellini' meanwhile shadows each de-briefing
Noonday in the *Black Bull* bar-café
Here behind the Trevi
Half-hidden by its atomising spray
He dreams nocturnal dancers
Timeless sensualities of water
Two who dance immortal – unrestrained
As we are two –

We also have our dreams

# Marcus Aurelius: Sixties Icon

You know the sort of open-air event –
A stately park become gymnasium
Free love   free hate   and horsemeat on a bun
The audience tricked out to be the show
The band inject their overdose of watts –
Black-clad panel-beaters out of Brum
Immune to their behemoth decibels
One poet in a man-dress bottled off
For not contributing to tinnitus

The sixties caravan just lumbered on –
Quite harmless impure psychotropic drugs
Effecting curt lobotomies of sex from love
And other narcissistic executions

Meanwhile above a pint of *London Pride*
Serge Gainsbourg and Jane Birkin
Studying the *Chelsea Potter* crowd
Begged if I might intercede a line
Of stoic rectitude
Embellishing their tape-looped heavy breathing

I brush aside a credit overdue
For *'Je t'aime – moi non plus'* –
But still you might recall a piquant line
Delivered in that *Franglais* redolent
Of Gainsboug's double-meanings –

'Physical love is a *cul-de-sack*
Mere sex a one-way street'

You do?    Me neither

# European Tour

Look at this man –
He's been up now three days and nights
What does he think he might miss
Conforming to nature's design?

His was the 'voice of a generation' –
And passing time accordingly displaced him –
A troubadour lauded as poet
By the twang of his sardonic lyre

At midnight his conversation
Veers from vision into thought-disorder
Why can't the poor man sleep?
What further expectation comes to haunt him?

A never-ending tour of far-flung theatres
Stadiums   Arenas –
To sing for his fanatics likewise ageing
Darkly smitten by misplaced nostalgia

For if ever there was a poet
Who might deliver continuous truth
My old gnarled tree in the garden
Has lived on unregarded

# Marcus Aurelius Discourses on Vintage Guitars

The real guitar exists within your mind –
No-one is the Maker
But soul and sweat of experience
The beautiful terrible memories –

If you allow all this into your hands
Your fingertips and grip – it is no matter
Maestro if you fail as a musician

Whatever you touch will bloom
Because such simple discipline
Brings you to the unity of all things

Patience with persistent application –
These are not among the modern virtues
And what are they but crass desire of fame?

This wood and wire you call your instrument
This Gibson Gold Top 1954 –

I'll take it with me now to pay your drug debts

# Marcus Aurelius Rehab

You'll not attain to Ecstasy
Getting wasted at a weekend rave
Nor mapping labyrinths of legal highs
One step ahead of legislation

Living on the edge
Of reason and remorse
Acolytes of Bacchus
Morpheus and crew
Flirt with a perpetual adolescence

Experience is what you get
Pursuing your desire
Then winding up with nothing –
At first that won't sink in
So try it once again

Same result?
You just might be a man
Beginning to turn inward –
But if you try and try
You tie yourself to habits
That sabotage the spirit

Lose control by all means –
Lose *yourself*
Though not by any chemical nor potion
Esoteric practice nor technique –
But take a sacred attitude to life
That means you're not the centre

What harms the hive
Is no good for the bee

# Marcus Aurelius and the Chinese Trade Delegation

Give me fire-works silk-worms and ice-cream
For I am an Italian

Incense noodles and the folding screen
For these I pay due tribute to Confucius

Dominoes and playing-cards and jade
You really are ingenious

Paper yen inspire my speculation –
Every man a millionaire in sprightly-coloured lire

Rice to make risotto   toilet rolls   meanwhile
A bristle toothbrush toyed with between meals

Mannequins and automatons
Soybeans and tuned bells

Chopsticks for ceramics
Cups and teapots conjured in transparent porcelain

Puppet theatres and the pontoon bridge
The kite and revolving bookcase

Let's celebrate in fortified rice wine –
Though there's another side I must examine

This undeniable delicacy
Has a darker application –

That poison-tipped repeating crossbow frame
Your frequent recourse to chemical warfare –

With bellows   mustard-smoke   and lime
Would you blow upon and blind my honest legions?

Let me give you in return
A Roman Wall that's wide as half the world

Please stay behind it –
At least until you're civilized

## Rest & Recreation

My soldiers were simply on holiday
They strayed across your border
For purely aesthetic purpose –

To rinse their hair in the *Rheinfalls*
To observe its iridescent
Rainbows cast from atomising spray

When later you discovered them cavorting
In slalom races   sliding on their shields
Up and down the *Rigi*

Frivolities as these might hardly cause distress
Would you not insist in sinister speculation
Of tactical reconnaissance preceding an invasion

Accepting these assurances
Please release my men   whose sensitivity
Waxes temperamental when confined

Accomplishing a duty of escape
Without regard to property or lives

## Bathing at Baden

Centurions while confiscating Switzerland
Built their citadel beside this spa –
Nostalgically impressed no doubt
By Nero's chic aquatic palaces –

The poolside bell has rung
And we must keep pace with its clock –
Moving from one muscle-toning jet
Into the next – strategically
Massaged by their warm salt-minerals

A thermal spring uniting opposites –
To bathe outdoors when snow descends the pines
Is quaint delight surreal as Baked Alaska –
Towelling robes perpetually warm
Kenya coffee warbling in its pot
Invite us to vacate a second womb
To be reborn?  Or sceptically
Re-read the *Zurich News*

We are that latest Lazarus –
Ex-pats decayed by taxes
Our camels having stretched the Needle's Eye
Of keyhole laser treatment
Cardio-vascular innovation

We take the air of floral chocolate
Strolling by our Alpine bovine meadow
Of Interlaken Elysium –

And raising eyes to spiritual peaks
We calculate no loss at the casino

# Roman Leave

Soldiers back in barracks are constrained
From open talk of politics
Not to mention merits of their gods
What do they discuss?
Poetry of course –
Being code for both of the above

They do not take restraint in verse
To signify conservative opinion
Nor Celtic wildness to denote
Anti-establishment freedom

But when on leave
They sample drinking dens
Then salons of those invitation-only
Bashes for promotion of new books

Hardship and attendant disappointment
Prepare them for bohemia's striptease –
That over-rated sideshow of civilian avoidance
Those skirmishes where only egos bleed

## Marcus Aurelius: Mentor

Young poet whom no publisher
Has deigned yet to publish
Do not be distressed
You might be blessed
Blocked from racking your soul
With arrant egocentricity

For in that endless sea
Of those who are now published
Fathomless infinite libraries rise and fall
Must you see their slender volumes
So many doors excluding your new voice?
You imagine they have glory –
But how many have you met?

Anxious in renown they fear a fall
Once more to obscurity – the forest floor
Where bashful nature's creatures
Have but one ambition –
Not to be noticed at all
For the swivelling eye of the predator
Welcomes silly fledglings to his larder

And they are dead
Who once could feel
The centre of their galaxy
As images   ideas   and rhythms swirled

It was only a foaming wave
Brilliantly basting a pebble
White for a while in the winter sun
Of a grey sea shelf

The gaudier their flag
The greater death's denial
You have no cause to envy this condition

Turn your metal-detector along the shore
You will stumble on such trash
As questions every man who called it treasure

# The Games

Caesar struck a silver coin
To celebrate the gladiator
*Rocky of Balboa*
Such being public acclaim

For years his name
Appeared high on the walls
Of taverns promising
Their strongest wine

He'd no desire of fame
Nor fear of death apparently
But entered *the lists* a slave
And left a Roman citizen

With vineyards and estates
The pension of an actor –
One who serves the State
As diplomat and orator

I'll not enumerate his mass
Of grievous wounds and lesions
*Vox populi* accordingly
May call my verse 'effete'

# Marcus Aurelius at the Cenotaph

I have no use for grandiose procession
Victors in a war are unimpressed
By anything save universal sadness
While that an eager populace expects
May differ by degree – intoxicants
Such as the siege and slaughter of a foe
Make only a non-combatant trip out
On patriotic fervour

Our nausea we swallow back until
Safely back in barracks we can spew
Indignation that the landless poor
Courageous young – and untried soldier
Suffer on all sides in times of war

Those who seek revenge
Can build two coffins –
One might house our shared humanity
You kill now at a distance – but despatched
To total up the damage
Find a face familiar as your own
Amid the butcher's block that was a town

I do not care to go to war at all
But if I must I wear a black armband
As going to the funeral of a friend
Forgive me if I keep my armband on
Two or three years more
Beyond our sacred victory celebration
This is Sicilian custom and tradition

## Marcus Aurelius: A Long Campaign

Enemies are predictable

Beware those who
Overwhelmingly
Admire you

They have a greater need
To set you underfoot –
Of all they once esteemed
To make a doormat

They style it 'progress' –
Over-zealous goals
Tantalizing targets
All seem to require
Relentless re-assessment

What better way
If you cannot ascend
Than to tarnish and trample
Those once revered?

See the bloom
Of reflected prestige
Dim and dissolve
From their gaze

Now they scan
By the lens of their age
But when

Did disdain
Contempt
Ambition

Amount to anything
But poison?

How they avoid your path
Now you are of the past

Then come into that citadel
Where only the ancients speak
Who earned their salt experience
By self-examination

## Gregory's Corso

*Caffe Vineria, Campo de' Fiori*

Academics   Gregory
Chop out lines to suit their pedantry
Sustain dishonest industry
Vying for outlandish variation
Their critical gimmicks
Ever more lucrative

I sense they dislike the lyric
From which they chew their bread
While lyrical poets living
Simply blunt their way
To sharper practice –
We are inconvenient peasants
Prizing one last field
Of rocks in the face of developers

None of them can claim
A poet from their ancestry
Rather they'd one eye upon a tenure
The moment their milk teeth sank into a steak

Take a long cold look on all their works
As they would grant us from their dry disdain

Now here come the priests
How very sleek –
In days preceding Holy Week
They line up in the barber's on this street
One whose radio bawls perpetual opera
He cuts their hair most carefully for free
Why? They appear on Vatican T. V.
Evidence of his pious handiwork –
He thinks it worth a fortnight of novenas

We poets are as poignantly deluded –
Giving to the Gatekeepers our final sheaf of wheat
Believing they'd distribute to the street

## Villa Borghese

One Roman spring you learnt the 'the facts of life'
Their green days are all past
Should you recant?

Replace them with observable truth:
Spring – Summer – Autumn – Winter
*These* are the facts of life

Whose circuit brought you here
One tramstop nearer paradise

Colourful train
On a rickety track
Round and round like a child's toy

So tell me now
If not now   when
Might a man seize hold of his life?

# Idioms of March

It ill becomes a man of my estate
To have no vices –
You need not be so proud
Concerning a mere accident of birth

If you were born to vices of this city
Where nothing's ever quite as it appears –

You are served a delicious peach
Which upon examination
Becomes a coloured marzipan
Sculpted to a ball

Surely this is worth the tasting
Where can be the harm?

But artifice becomes a habit
Then an expectation

This can lead to downfall
Suspecting those sincere
Of insincerity

A pat upon the shoulder
Does not mean
A dagger in the back

'Have a nice day' on the other hand –
Whatever can they mean?
Is this day to be my last?

# The Spanish Steps

John Keats was not 'himself' that day
Ambling out to Highgate on the Heath
His little rifle only fit for larking
Braced in one bunched shoulder
Knocked cock-robin off a branch red-breasted
'I think I'll pack in the medical game'

To end up renting rooms
So near The Spanish Steps
Each pilgrim footfall fired
Mood-swings to his T. B. raddled nerves

Idealised portraiture
Toned down his tough exterior
Unrequited ardour
Gave an early death romantic glamour

'Written on water'? Nothing more?
Came Forensics on the scene
'Take his DNA and have the lab-boys run it down'

A kink in his museum locket-hair
Discloses tincture of cannabis
Opium   laudanum   cocaine-tonic
All legally acquired   (historically of course)
From Haverstock Hill's dispensing late-night chemist

# Marcus Aurelius: Historian

Sand dunes drift across Sahara
Covering sand dunes formed before
Concealing the past in sand we assume
Constitutes permanent landscape and form

This way history fails to give warning
To blinkered men mired in their time –
For whom compassion to those departed
A mere year ago is a footnote too far –

Are they departed?   Are we so sure
We walk with the living and touch what is real?
Or conjured from sand is this but a dream
We put on our work-clothes vainly pursuing?

Ours is the mirage rising from dust –
Cast modest eyes on the ghost of the world
Its shifting pattern of border and rule
Of herds and of armies   masses and markets

For there's no such thing as a good-natured camel
His neck is contrived to turn on the rider
Rending and tearing just as the mood takes him –

The past we forget will return to devour

# Marcus Aurelius is from Mars

Have you seen my legions dance
Ecstatically in full regalia?

Have you seen them
Seamlessly
Raise their wall of shields
Into a blinding river
Formed of silver fish-scales?

The shawms and bagpipes
Of our foes grow silent
Today it is
The festival of Mars

# Conquest

Having subdued the natives
Quite to his satisfaction
And dreaming of an imminent promotion
He mistook a sleeping lion for a sand dune
Delivering one quick kick
So hard his sandal sailed into the air

This prevented running very far

An obstacle placed squarely on the path
As picaresque displacement to a journey
Is better accepted surely

Than to elevate one's status prematurely
Above its guiding providence

# One Small Room

He came to this poor quarter of the city
Seeking one small room at meagre rent

Now a plaque is placed above the door –
A poet of these streets once ill-esteemed

To celebrate his lifetime gift for friendship
Who served a Christian muse of fortitude

Obituaries all praised his well-made verse
But could not see beyond the one small room

'Sordid and squalid' they called it
Imputing his search for love the same

They live in rooms far smaller –
Their offices of prurient assumption

The undivided world of imagination
That was where he lived and worked

And they cannot contain him
Reduce him to one small room

Who has entered that vast embrace
A poet sings towards across a lifetime

# Spiritus

Do you love the greater good
Or a small convenient idol in a shed?

I do not mean your sportive
Mid-life crisis red Ferrari –
Fetish of a potent nature sprite

But when you speculate upon the world
That always gives short shrift
Constantly manipulating
Counterweights and measures in its shop

You'll have enough insurance dividend
Only if your 'ship' stays in dry dock

That snowflakes fall
By myriad design
Suggests they have a destiny
Though meltingly temporal
Beyond desire to simply co-inhere –
As if creation were in love
With diverse individuation

The gods are gathering and throwing gravel
Up to your shuttered bedroom window
The gods who awake to incite uncertain journeys
Neither angels   demons   nor your friends
They are rather agency nurses
Tasked with assertive outreach on your soul

# Men at Work

Slapdash city
Approach roads pot-holed and pitted
*Londinium*
Though not as we left it –

Your gaff's a kennel in Camden Town?
Back in the day
You'd have full under-floor heating
But your council took it out
To form a communal sewer
Of polluted River Fleet

There's no respect
The whole shebang
Gone to the (isle of) dogs

It would take a Thames tsunami
To retro-fit your city to our plan –

First the concrete must contain
Volcanic ash and fresh spring water
To form those microscopic
Fast-binding crystal hydrates
That over time
Will stop all cracks from spreading –

Smooth surfaces you'll see
Resistant to corrosion
Like this bust
Of youthful Apollo
The Face
Of eternal Rome

# Excavation

They worshipped Bacchus
Mercury and Venus –
Not by any roadside shrine
But Soho's sacred site

On dreamtime's licensed premises
They praised their poets dead
When lacking this condition
Were seen to tolerate
Scars from dislocation
Of the spirit and the mind
Invisible flaws became
Acceptable stigmata

And did they care for art
While caring very little for themselves?
That question might endanger the enquirer –
Their long dark bars in aftermath
Of sick regret and callous disregard
Sanctified bohemian adherence
Where fortune only bloomed
To haunt a sad decline

And did they love each other?
Carnally the evidence is clear –
Each presumed the lead role in a play
All others dimly lit upon their stage –
Often in a wine-lodge matinee
Struggling with a few allotted lines
Mood-swings used a wrecking ball
To improvise

## Marcus Aurelius: On Love

This world will dissolve like snow
Your personal world
Ever more swiftly passes –
Suddenly outside all space and time
You stand before the Creator –
'What have you done with love?'–
This being His main medium

Love was not invented in my time
There were so many words for this
None took it quite as seriously

Instead we searched for Truth –
Our ethical symposiums
Accompanied by much wine
Often ended in debauchery

You have no such excuse
You are like a man who says
'I saved so many frogs and mice
And birds and long-legged flies' –
Of course you did –
Because you kept a cat!

You only save someone
You have not first exposed to terror –
Love without ambivalence might be
Beyond your animal nature

How unprepared you are
For the ultimate pertinent question –
Let me suggest an antidote
In a world of change and chance
Metaphysics play the minor part

Repeat after me
The meaning of love is food
On this planet of inequity
Love commends one action –
You must nurture one another

## A Foreign Country

We disembark
To Britain's bracing climate –
Cashconverters   Poundshops
Scored discarded Scratchcards
Foodbank fodder   Charity couture

Theme Park for a working poor

Bacchus is un-worshipped in binge-drinking
Lads and Ladettes shout
Then piss about the market square –
Banished gods return as new diseases

Health Services hit targets
But meanwhile miss the point –

That which can be measured
So often counts for nothing
When that which counts immeasurably
Is held of no account

# Drusilla

'They keep coal in the bath
Not that they bathe
But go all year in goose-grease undergowns'

Learning I'd be stationed here
From one of her ex-squaddies in the Med.
Drusilla gave her quaint idea of Briton

'In winter they must share a bed with sheep
While cattle wander in their living room'
Her lowdown on Londinium followed suit

'They make you eat eel pie
Topped by an emerald vomit
Fished from Father Thames
And you shall retch it back there double quick –
It's ante-room to Hades'

But I might say
It beats the brutal sunstroke
Handed out by Carthage
Or dodging Goth atrocities
All along the Danube into Linz –
Besides I have a lucky phallic pendant
Engraved to read
'An upright man of Rome'

Drusilla gave it me
All the while asserting
She's no man's property
Nor wishes for a steady male admirer

I'll soldier with the Task Force into Wales
Until that girl sees sense –
One day we'll open up a pizza joint
In a corner of Trastevere
Where pine trees lend a shade

One window for an outlet to the street
We'll treble business by the passing trade
And my cousin Rocco breeds the best
Black olives in Emilia-Romagna

## Patrol

Impulsive youth – a severed hand
One foot beneath our feet
Then here his headless corpse

You never know on whom the gods may smile

Tribes that trouble Rome
Attribute occult power
To hacked-off heads
They hoist them by the hair

And so to charm our border guard
Post them on their poles of holy juju

Imagining we'd lose our rag
Rampage through their forest
Blunder stupefied by grief
Upon their favoured skewer-pits
Spring-loaded for kebab

Soberly the truth is this
We wait
We wait until there is *no time*
We wait until the order comes

'Close combat – give no quarter'

## Policy Application

Intemperate executioners are allowed
Too much licence I submit
Following our recent insurrection

While they have their private joke
Refining a straightforward crucifixion
Nailing scrotum sacs and ears unnecessarily

It might not take much measure of persuasion
Should one condemned insist
They nail him upside down

That he should not appear to
Approach in form of punishment
The despatch of his late master

A pretender to Judea's throne
For which in purple duster
Briar crown and brushwood sceptre

He learned firsthand those jocular
Conceptions I have outlined
To which as yet no policy pertains

## The Temple at Jerusalem

Determined not to dream
She takes a sleeping draught –
How long ago it seems
She saw the sphere of light
Perceiving it contained
All events on earth
All past and future things
In one vertiginous wave –
And was she then asleep
Or lifted beyond time?

The cosmos bore a human outline
And when they brought the prisoner in
He seemed as present yet removed
All the while her consort searched the truth
By philosophical dialogue –
But the prisoner would have none of it
Refusing abstract thought

She had lingered in this city far too long
Absorbing antiquated superstition –
The ark that lived unseen inside its unrecorded room
The hidden circuits of the inner temple
The want of transparent truth
A constant source of unrest with Roman rule

Her dreams had passed their crisis now
And should one prisoner go free
Might history subside to spare
More hapless martyrs in its endless sphere?
The sphere of light containing time and space
Its hideous powers and movements
Too numerous for any human mind?

## Marcus Aurelius: Astronomer

When you see by radio telescope
Double-helix circles round a death star
Pause to re-consider
One thousand light years have already passed

The blinking of your eye might add
Another lifetime's interlude –
So put an end to sorrow

It is seldom worth your while
And put an end to joy
There is nothing to get worked up about
But you risk a sober mind
Circling both extremes like a gad-fly
Whose fruits are inconsiderable

A gad-fly with a tail
One thousand light years long
Gone in the blink of an eye

Instead take hold of your mood –
Your lips as warm as snow
Have vowed to love forever
While your thoughts re-hash old enmities
From extinct invisible foes

The stars do not speak our language
And cannot reason with themselves –
Volatile mineral gases
Hotheads and burnt-out creatives
Who consider their birth and passing
Of inflated importance to human affairs

# Chet: 'Summer Sketch'

In the city of Bologna
There's a jazz club bears his name
So typically of course
He never played there

Preferring one without a sign
That mainly serves spaghetti

A summer concert in the square
Returning here for supper
He drew a portrait sketch upon the menu
One continuous line
In the manner of Matisse or Cocteau or
Chet Baker when he circles a white space
With notes of calm allusive beauty

Whose is this suggested face at peace
They promptly framed and hung upon the wall?

Could it be a somnolent
Self-sabotaging angel
Sleepwalking fame's absurd fast-burning tightrope?

## Maggiore

Silent walls surround our ancient family –
Absence of pronouncement in the press
Our safely irreproachable dark dress –
Such lives avoid the taint of ostentation

Abjuring webs of monetary transgression
(The lake is placid where a sail expires)
We've tacked beyond the breeze of all desire
Nor give occasion to the world for envy –

A facile sense that some have found a haven
Without responsibility or fault
(Our family crypt contains a secret vault)
Old money has humility of purpose

Meetings shall of course be kept to time
Your quiet tie suggests you have the gist
Regrettably the Rolex tags your wrist
As someone yet removed from subtle battle

True samurai need hardly show the sword
To indicate all status is distraction
We hope we have begun your education
We trust your stay remains a mystery

# Marcus Aurelius: On Impiety

Those concrete-thinkers having won the day
Have filled your every day with concrete
You have been conned
You cannot hear the corncrake
Rising from the wildflower meadow
The fields are full of rape

They professed to be Romans
They said 'we build a Roman road
Hard-evidenced in scientific fact'
All that is soft they suspected
Then since it may not be measured
They tied the heart in a Gordian knot

Do you think they are Romans?
You have been conned –
Apollo source of light
Has their celestial measurement
He circumscribes their stars
And stares into their lack of feeling

This is the arrow in his bow
Poised to strike at will –
It is of their own making
Madmen drunk on fact
Denying their own miracle –
Impiety disowning play
Of eternal cosmic opposites

# The Animals Preach to St. Francis

Prelates of your Church
Dissemble and decline
To say that we possess eternal souls

Birds of the air and Lilies of the field
Were good enough to serve as metaphor
When you renounced your father's fashion-house
To be a teenage hippy in these hills

Let us reconsider who it was
Carried his fruits of labour
Transported to foreign parts
Those bales of rag-trade *schmutter*
You gracelessly abandoned
To form a Brotherhood

Holy little rich boy
Persuade the Holy See
Every pet co-habiting man's house
Inspires a pure affection

This can lead (at last) to sacred love
An impulse of compassion
Your own eccentric species seems to lack toward its brother

# Fontana

A fountain throws itself away
Water is theology
Its spray
Erodes the world's
Psychopathic sanity

As through the rainbow
Falls the rain
On you as on your enemy

Water falls
Through law and book
Rivers leap
Before they look

And fish have reached
The Vatican
Proposing new
Jerusalem

## Duchessa

Her mind is in another room
There you may not follow
Never should you quite attain
Its long-established climate

You are unborn   untutored here
Where privilege subsumes itself
Fortune means you no offence
Do not deny your nervousness

But let us speak of timeless themes
Anodyne voluptuous
Present time suspends its truth
Her humour has that modest deprecation –

But put away all greater expectation
Collect yourself with coffee – recollect
A river brown with finance flows between you
Your rooms are rented from the circumspect

# Paper Dagger

Machiavelli advised the Prince
'Hand to your associates
A secret paper dagger –

Choose a *fictional* failing
Have it known
Such a theme of weakness or remorse
Hurls you helplessly
Into intemperate mood –
That you no longer function
Fight nor reason
But are a malleable person

See who will
Draw from his sleeve
This paper-soft stiletto
Wielding its imagined slight
As if to find the heart

Might you call him 'friend'?
Many a friend of princes
Conceals such seed of enmity –

Then furnish them all
With harmless paper daggers
That point towards their own hearts
When unsheathed'

But regarding Health & Safety
Today we might append:
'This is a pure device of paranoia
Not without its danger to the user
So please proceed with caution and
*Do not try this at home*'

## Marcus Aurelius is Not Proud

The world is simple
Only man
Maddened by his appetites
Prefers a hell of endless disappointment –

What might satisfy?
He feeds on everything as if in famine?

A pageant   a farce   a new romance
All novelties –
What selfish impulse sets his course
Ajar like wooden puppetry?

Until his thoughts are anchored in regret
He tramples flowers before him unreflecting –

For flowers now interpose his fellow man –
Not put here for his usury
Nor animals designed
As walking delicatessen

But he must have rule over them

And so his outlook grows mechanical
Pursuing new obsession
To companion his conceit –

Pride that prides itself
On being free from pride –
Isn't this the more sinister?
Politicians crawl into that pot-hole
Dragging their retinue with them
Then cripple the whole population
Overtaxing the poorest poor –

'Such briars are good for you
Instilling a Spartan spirit'
Say those whose pious practice is
The vice of self-flagellation

# Prolific

As long as you are composing
You are not decomposing
You suppose

That must be the reason
– 32 books and counting –
Continuously you bare your soul

Attempting the longest chain letter
From any one man to his maker

I simply sent a love-note
– What's the hurry? –
On mule by second-class mail

Trusting the courts of heaven
Remain un-swayed by ceaseless chanting

## Bay of Lindos

There are so many gods
To help you kneel
To help you squat or sit
To tie yourself in knots
To task yourself
With duties and devotions

gods you love to fear
and gods you fear to love –

Where is the god
To say 'Stand up'
'Stand up and walk away
From this ungodly enervating sickness'?

# A Provincial Assizes

'Please go home and reason with yourself' –
The presiding magistrate   resisting undue haste
'Take a fortnight to resume
Your tribute to the gods of Rome
Your oath to Caesar crowned a living god
From whom your service-discharge bread and wine
Commends your past allegiance bearing arms'

Why sanction execution of a soldier
Drawn into that slaves' pernicious cult
Deemed to stem from one dead Nazarene?

Make precedent of liberal jurisprudence –
Marcus Aurelius counselled as much
Finding something yet to admire
In youthful alienation
Scrawling chalk graffiti of small fish
On pavements by the Apian Gate –
'A puerile imitation of the stoics'
He summarised their interesting creed

Rome of course was harder pressed
Its jails were jammed with martyrs –
'Why not loop a rope around your neck
And step out from a precipice?'
One judiciary advised them –
An exasperating problem!

He blamed the schismatic Gnostics
For insisting that their Jeshu never suffered
Nor died   nor lived again –
It was all to be perceived *symbolically* you see –
But only by trained adepts such as they!

Result? – a disturbed minority
Volunteer to be free lunch
In the Coliseum's – hideously expensive –
Abyssinian lions' jaws

# Cinecitta

The film plays to an empty theatre

Time elapses –
Now the audience enters

They try to ascertain the plot –
Vineyards seas and cities
Fact and dream collide and intermingle –
Unlikely heroes raise applause
Also bears and horses –

Comedy misfortune interlude for kisses

The beginning still unseen –
So pivotal to the plot

'It is after many wars' some say
'It is after climate change'
'It is spiritual evolution'

Some claim to have the original print
'Encoded in DNA'
'No – it is learned and acquired'
'Mere chemicals inside a cosmic egg'

Absorbed by the film
They forget a former existence
Beyond the cinema door

Then one by one they leave
The film still runs
They never see its ending

The film plays to an empty theatre

Time elapses –
Now the audience enters

## Marcus Aurelius Offers Solace

In a very little while
You will be scattered ashes
Or a skeleton
Having fed the worms

Then be of good cheer –
Whatever hardship
Turn of fortune
Failure in worldly success
Accompanies this –
Your superannuated corpse –
Surely it is not
So difficult to bear

Some follow funerals
Some obituaries
Then tell themselves
How glad they are to be alive –
They are only half-deluded
Pass the funeral port
It comforts those
Apprentices
At others' heartfelt mourning

When we look upon our generation
Perceiving the scythe grows nearer
Our own small patch of grass
There is a frisson –
Not without pleasure –
Of suspended annihilation

'Doctors can be wrong…'
'This year I really shall…'
'Now I'll put my house in order…'
Stories mankind tells itself
Repeat these same few dramas

Once you searched for treasure
Some saw in you a prince
A flock of talking birds
Befriended you –
Where are those days fled
So soon   so very soon?

When you throw a peck of earth
As it were on your own coffin
Take my hand –
Your friend Marcus Aurelius –

History does not know
For never would I tell
But between you and me

Add a Roman pinch of elegiac poet

# Marcus Aurelius: Webpage

From Elysian groves I Google myself
In coffee shops of the garrulous dead
Who enjoy supernatural sight
Light-years beyond your wi-fi bounty
Accompanying an unpaid mid-day break's
Cinnamon-sprinkled low-fat skinny latte

How these specious scholars of the web
Have simplicated me –
Another ancient sanitised celeb.
Consigned to wicked-pedia

(Read my *Meditations* for the juice
And never trust a hippy)

I continue virtually at least
In bluffed and sweated schoolboy cribs
Their multi-trillion hits assuring me
Mathematical immortality

That when disordered government
Plants its citizen-chip
In every new-born brain
Fusing mini PC screens
To pairs of non-negotiable Gucci glasses

I shall be there to befriend you
Counselling against extremes
In a post-civilised culture
Whose ethos is to render
Every cowed consumer
Collectively bi-polar